NAVIGATING UNCERTAINTY

Navigating Uncertainty

Hichem Karoui

Copyright © 2024 by Hichem Karoui

Global East-West (London)

All rights reserved. No part of this book may be reproduced in any manner whatsoever without written permission except in the case of brief quotations embodied in critical articles and reviews.

First Printing, 2024

CONTENTS

1 - Introduction 1
- References 9
2 - The Global Geopolitical Tapestry 13
- References 21
3 - Evolving Dynamics Among Major World Powers 25
- References 35
4 - The Rise of New Powers 37
- References 43
5 - Emerging Global Powers 45
- References 53
6 - The Kaleidoscope of Global Powers 55
- References 69
7 - Geopolitical Metamorphosis . . . 71

- References 85
- Bibliography 89

1

INTRODUCTION

In an era of unprecedented global flux, the international geopolitical tapestry is being dramatically rewoven (Mearsheimer, 2018). Gone are the simple certainties of yesteryear. Today, the world stage bristles with complexity – new powers emerge, old alliances crack, and traditional players scramble to redefine their roles (Friedman, 2020). This isn't just politics as usual. No, it's an intricate dance of economics, social forces, cutting-edge technology, and military might, all colliding and collaborating to forge tomorrow's global order.

China's meteoric rise stands as perhaps the most stunning transformation of our time. Like a dragon awakening from ancient slumber, this Asian giant has not merely grown – it has exploded onto the world stage with breathtaking velocity (Shambaugh, 2021). The Belt and Road Initiative

(BRI), Beijing's ambitious masterstroke, stretches its fingers across continents like ancient silk routes reborn in steel and concrete (Huang, 2018). But China's reach extends far beyond infrastructure. In labs and research centers across the nation, Chinese scientists and engineers push the boundaries of AI and 5G technology (Baker, 2020), while in the South China Sea, territorial disputes simmer dangerously, threatening regional stability (Storey, 2020).

The United States, that towering colossus of the post-war order, finds itself at a crossroads. Within its borders, deep fissures have appeared. Short, sharp domestic conflicts erupt regularly (Pew Research Center, 2021). Long-held certainties crumble. Abroad, America's traditional role as a global shepherd faces unprecedented scrutiny, while its relationship with China has curdled into a complex brew of competition and interdependence (Bitzinger, 2019). The "America First" echoes still reverberate through diplomatic corridors, leaving allies uncertain and adversaries emboldened (Goldgeier, 2020).

Russia, that eternal enigma, prowls the global stage with renewed purpose. In Eastern Europe, its actions speak louder than words – Crimea annexed, Ukraine destabilized, Western relations in tatters (Nolan, 2021). Moscow's digital warriors wage shadow wars in cyberspace while its military forces project power from Syria to the Arctic (Cohen, 2018). Sometimes subtle, sometimes brutal, Russia's geopolitical chess moves demand the world's attention.

The Middle East remains a crucible of conflict, where ancient enmities and modern power plays create a volatile mix. Syria bleeds, Yemen suffers, and Iraq struggles to find its footing (Roberts, 2019). Iran and Saudi Arabia circle each other like wary predators, while global powers—some with good intentions, others perhaps less so—meddle in regional affairs (Gause, 2019). Through it all, the Israeli-Palestinian conflict endures a seemingly eternal flame that continues to shape regional politics and global diplomacy (Baker, 2022).

The European Union, once a shining exemplar of unity and cross-border harmony, now finds itself navigating treacherous waters. Brexit crashed through the bloc like a tidal wave, leaving behind a wake of uncertainty and strained relationships (Wright, 2020). In some corners of the continent, nationalism rears its head—a stubborn phoenix rising from the ashes of past conflicts (Judt, 2019). The EU, caught between its lofty aspirations and harsh realities, must somehow thread the needle between maintaining internal cohesion and projecting global influence, all while waves of migration lap at its shores and global powers circle like hungry sharks (Fletcher, 2021).

The Asia-Pacific theater crackles with tension. Here, titans clash—America's established might versus China's surging ambition—in a high-stakes game of influence and power (Hamprecht, 2021). The South China Sea boils with competing claims while ASEAN members perform a delicate diplomatic dance (Liu, 2020). India, that sleeping giant, has awakened with renewed purpose, throwing its considerable weight around the regional chessboard (Pant, 2022). Short, sharp confrontations alternate with long periods of uneasy détente. Military vessels prowl contested waters. Fighter jets test boundaries. Alliances shift like desert sands (Goh, 2021).

Turn your gaze to Africa and Latin America, where the next chapter of global politics is written in real-time. Africa's vast resources—its minerals glittering like promises in the earth—have sparked a new scramble for influence (Woods, 2020). China's Belt and Road Initiative snakes across the continent, building literal and metaphorical bridges (Zhang, 2019). In Latin America, old paradigms crumble as new alignments emerge (Meyer,

2020). Brazil and Mexico, regional powerhouses, flex their diplomatic muscles while navigating between Beijing's entreaties and Washington's expectations (Dussel, 2021).

The future of global institutions hangs precariously in the balance. Traditional pillars of international order – the UN, WTO, EU – creak under the weight of mounting challenges (Zürn, 2020). Nationalism surges, then retreats, then surges again (Riemann, 2021). Some leaders embrace isolation while others champion interconnectedness. The old rules-based order bends, but will it break? Global challenges mount: climate change threatens to redraw coastlines and reshape economies, while pandemics remind us of our shared vulnerability (IPCC, 2021).

In this volatile mix, the Arctic emerges as tomorrow's geopolitical hotspot. As ice sheets retreat, revealing new shipping routes and resource deposits, nations jockey for position in this emerging frontier (Hoffman, 2022). Climate change, that great destabilizer, reshapes more than coastlines—transforming international relations (Kelley, 2020). The COVID-19 pandemic delivered a stark lesson in global interdependence (Baker, 2021), showing how quickly local crises can spiral into worldwide catastrophes. Through it all, the world's powers must somehow find ways to cooperate even as they compete, build even as they contest, and preserve even as they pursue change.

In the labyrinthine field of modern geopolitics, where power dynamics shift like desert sands, we witness an unprecedented transformation of the global order. With its ambitious Belt and Road Initiative, China's meteoric rise collides with America's established hegemony—a dance of titans reverberating across continents. Meanwhile, Russia's strategic maneuvers in Eastern Europe and beyond paint a complex tableau of influence and resistance.

The Middle East remains a crucible of competing interests, where ancient rivalries intertwine with modern power plays (Peters, 2020). In Brussels, the European Union grapples with internal fissures while striving to maintain its relevance on the world stage (Brunner, 2021). The Asia-Pacific theater pulses with tension as territorial disputes and economic competition create a delicate balance of power (Doran, 2022).

Emerging from historical shadows, Africa and Latin America increasingly assert their influence, reshaping traditional power dynamics (Krastev, 2021). Traditional alliances bend and flex under new pressures, while international institutions struggle to adapt to 21st-century challenges (Väyrynen, 2021). Climate change and global health crises transcend borders, forcing unlikely collaborations and testing established diplomatic frameworks.

This intricate tapestry of global relations demands nuanced understanding. Some nations forge ahead with bold initiatives, while others carefully calibrate their responses to shifting circumstances. Through this complex interplay of cooperation and competition, humanity charts its course through uncertain waters, where every action ripples across an interconnected world of competing interests, shared challenges, and evolving alliances.

References

- Baker, A. (2020). *A new era in technology and geopolitics*. The Atlantic.
- Baker, A. (2021). *Pandemic politics and global interdependence*. Foreign Affairs.
- Bitzinger, R. (2019). *The US-China trade war: A complicated relationship*. Journal of International Affairs.
- Brunner, E. (2021). *The EU's relevance in a multipolar world*. European Council on Foreign Relations.
- Cohen, A. (2018). *Russia's cyber warfare strategies*. Hoover Institution.
- Doran, M. (2022). *Contemporary security dynamics in the Asia-Pacific*. Strategic Studies Quarterly.
- Dussel, E. (2021). *Latin America in a new geopolitical landscape*. Inter-American Dialogue.
- Fletcher, M. (2021). *Nationalism in Europe: The rise of the far-right*. The Guardian.
- Friedman, G. (2020). *The coming chaos in geopolitics*. Geopolitical Futures.
- Gause, F.G. (2019). *The Iranian-Saudi rivalry: Implications for the region*. Foreign Affairs.
- Goh, E. (2021). *ASEAN's role in regional stability*. Asian Survey.
- Goldgeier, J. (2020). *America's role in the world amidst political divides*. Brookings Institution.
- Hamprecht, J. (2021). *US-China tensions in the Indo-Pacific*. Pacific Affairs.
- Hoffman, M. (2022). *The Arctic in a warming world: Geopolitical tensions rise*. Journal of Arctic Policy.

- Huang, Y. (2018). *Belt and Road Initiative: Strategy and outlook*. China Quarterly.
- IPCC (2021). *Climate Change 2021: The Physical Science Basis*. Intergovernmental Panel on Climate Change.
- Judt, T. (2019). *Nationalism and its disturbing revival*. The New York Review of Books.
- Kelley, A. (2020). *Climate change and its effects on geopolitics*. Center for Climate and Security.
- Krastev, I. (2021). *The new geopolitics of Africa and Latin America*. European Council on Foreign Relations.
- Liu, C. (2020). *Sovereignty disputes in the South China Sea*. Asian Journal of International Relations.
- Meyer, C. (2020). *Latin America's shifting geopolitical landscape*. Latin American Politics and Society.
- Mearsheimer, J. (2018). *The Great Delusion: Liberal Dreams and International Realities*. Yale University Press.
- Nolan, C. (2021). *Russia and the West: A new Cold War?*. International Affairs Review.
- Pant, H.V. (2022). *India's emergent role in South Asia*. The Diplomat.
- Peters, A. (2020). *The Israeli-Palestinian conflict: Enduring divisions and potential for peace*. Foreign Policy.
- Pew Research Center. (2021). *Political polarization in the U.S.*.
- Riemann, H. (2021). *The rise of populism in Western democracies*. Journal of Political Ideologies.
- Roberts, D. (2019). *Understanding the Middle East conflicts*. Middle East Institute.
- Shambaugh, D. (2021). *China's global role and ambitions*. Foreign Affairs.
- Storey, I. (2020). *The South China Sea: U.S.-China rivalry and regional implications*. Journal of Asian Security and International Affairs.
- Väyrynen, R. (2021). *Global governance in a multipolar world*. Global Governance Journal.

- Wright, T. (2020). *Brexit and its implications for the EU.* European Politics and Society.
- Woods, N. (2020). *Africa's geopolitical significance in a global context.* African Affairs.
- Zhang, T. (2019). *The Belt and Road Initiative and Africa's future.* China-Africa Research Initiative.

2

THE GLOBAL GEOPOLITICAL TAPESTRY

A COMPLEX WEB OF POWER AND INFLUENCE

Snap! The world order shifts again. In today's lightning-paced global arena, understanding geopolitics isn't just smart—it's survival. Think of it as a grand chess match where every move ripples across continents, where Twitter diplomacy meets ancient territorial disputes, and where economic warfare can strike harder than missiles (Friedman, 2020).

China's rise? It's breathtaking. Beijing isn't just building roads—it's rewriting the rules of global engagement (Shambaugh, 2021). The Belt and Road Initiative snakes across continents like a dragon's tail, leaving gleaming ports and high-speed rails in its wake (Huang, 2018). But make no mistake: this isn't mere infrastructure. It's power projection, pure and simple. Meanwhile, in the South China Sea, tension crackles like static before a storm (Storey, 2020). Aircraft carriers prowl while fishing boats play cat-and-mouse games with coast guards (Gao, 2021).

The United States—once the undisputed heavyweight champion of global influence—now finds itself in uncharted waters. Gone are the days of unchallenged American exceptionalism. The Trump presidency? That was just the tip of the iceberg (Bitzinger, 2019). Traditional allies now hedge their bets, cultivating new partnerships like gardeners preparing for winter (Goldgeier, 2020). Some call it decline; others call it evolution. The truth? It's complicated.

Russia! Now there's a plot twist. Putin's Russia plays geopolitical chess with a boxer's mindset. Crimea, Ukraine, Syria—each move calculated, each strategy layered with subterfuge (Cohen,

2018). Their cyber warriors strike from shadow realms, while energy politics freezes Europe into paralysis (Nolan, 2021). It's 19th-century power politics wearing 21st-century digital armor (Dmitriev, 2020).

The Middle East? Good grief—what a kaleidoscope of chaos! Ancient hatreds collide with modern ambitions. Oil flows while blood spills (Roberts, 2019). Every solution breeds ten new problems. ISIS may be diminished, but the ideological wildfire they ignited still smolders (Gause, 2019). Israel and Palestine remain locked in their eternal dance, while Iran and Saudi Arabia circle each other like wary prizefighters (Peters, 2020).

Here's the kicker: this isn't your grandfather's geopolitics. Quantum computing, artificial intelligence, and climate change are reshaping the battlefield (Kelley, 2020). Water wars loom. Digital currencies threaten to upend financial systems (Ghosh, 2021). Space isn't just for astronauts anymore—it's the new military high ground (NATO, 2022).

Get this straight: understanding these dynamics isn't optional. Whether you're a CEO in Singapore or a farmer in Sudan, global power plays will impact your life (Riemann, 2021). The world's becoming more connected, yet paradoxically more fractured. Alliances shift like desert sands. Today's friend? Tomorrow's rival.

In this brave new world, adaptability isn't just an asset—it's oxygen. The old rules are crumbling, and the new ones are being written in real-time (Mearsheimer, 2018). Keep your eyes open, your mind sharp, and your analysis fluid. Because in this grand game of power and influence, the only constant is change.

Remember: tomorrow's world order is being forged in today's crucible of chaos. Understanding it isn't just an academic exercise—it's a survival skill for the 21st century.

THE EVOLVING GEOPOLITICAL LANDSCAPE: A MULTIFACETED ANALYSIS

In an era of unprecedented global interconnectivity, the European Union's grand experiment in supranational governance teeters on a knife's edge. While this bold venture once symbolized the triumph of cooperation over conflict, it now faces staggering challenges that threaten to unravel decades of careful integration (Wright,

2020). Brexit struck like a thunderbolt, sending tremors through the continent's political foundations (Norris, 2022). Yet this departure, dramatic as it was, merely scratches the surface of the EU's deeper struggles.

Nationalism, that old European demon, has reared its head again. From Budapest to Warsaw, populist movements surge and recede like tides, leaving behind deposits of euroskepticism that corrode the bloc's foundations (Judt, 2019). The migration crisis—a humanitarian challenge of staggering proportions—has exposed raw nerves and deep fissures within the union (Fletcher, 2021). Some member states throw open their doors; others slam them shut.

The Asia-Pacific theater presents an entirely different spectacle, where China's meteoric rise collides with America's established hegemony (Liu, 2020). In the South China Sea's choppy waters, billion-dollar warships play an elaborate game of cat and mouse, while diplomatic cables buzz with barely concealed tensions (Doran, 2022). North Korea's nuclear saber-rattling adds a wild card to this high-stakes poker game, keeping military strategists awake at night and diplomats working overtime (Cohen, 2022).

Look to **Africa**, and you'll find a continent transformed (Meyer, 2020). Here, China's Belt and Road Initiative weaves through ancient trade routes, laying down fiber-optic cables alongside new railways (Zhang, 2019). Russian private military contractors patrol resource-rich regions, while Western nations watch with mounting concern (Pelham, 2020). The continent pulses with potential energy—economic, demographic, and political—yet old challenges of governance and development persist stubbornly (Williams, 2021).

Latin America's story unfolds in equally complex chapters. In the shadow of the United States, nations navigate between sovereignty and interdependence, prosperity and inequality (Dussel, 2021). Some countries embrace Chinese investment; others maintain traditional alignments. Political winds shift dramatically—from far-left to far-right and back again—while drug cartels and climate change ignore borders entirely (Meyer, 2020).

Global challenges demand global solutions, yet our international institutions creak under the weight of 21st-century problems (Zürn, 2020). The United Nations Security Council, designed for a post-World War II world, struggles to address modern crises (Friedman, 2021). Regional organizations spring up like mushrooms after rain, filling governance gaps but sometimes creating new complications.

The world watches as new powers rise and old alliances evolve. Technology reshapes warfare and diplomacy alike, while climate change threatens to redraw maps and resettle populations (Woods, 2020). In this kaleidoscopic landscape, the only constant is change itself—rapid, relentless, and often revolutionary.

To navigate these turbulent waters requires more than just traditional statecraft. It demands innovation in diplomacy, resilience in institutions, and perhaps most crucially, the wisdom to know when to compete and when to cooperate (Mearsheimer, 2021). As we peer into an uncertain future, one thing becomes crystal clear: the geopolitical challenges of tomorrow will require solutions as complex and interconnected as the problems themselves.

In this kaleidoscopic moment of global transformation, we witness an unprecedented convergence of challenges and possibilities that defies conventional geopolitical wisdom. Power itself has become fluid, flowing through digital networks as readily as through traditional channels, while the very notion of national sovereignty undergoes radical reimagining in an age of transnational corporations and borderless threats (Friedman, 2020). The old certainties—of American hegemony, of predictable alliances, of clear divisions between East and West—dissolve into a far more nuanced and volatile reality (Shambaugh, 2021).

Yet perhaps this very uncertainty signals not chaos, but evolution. Like a complex ecosystem adapting to environmental pressures, the international order self-organizes in fascinating and unexpected ways (Zürn, 2020). China's Belt and Road Initiative interweaves with Silicon Valley's digital dominance, while grassroots movements leverage social media to influence policy alongside traditional state actors (Kelley, 2020). Through this intricate dance of competing interests and collaborative necessities, a new world order emerges—not imposed from above, but growing organically from the dynamic interactions of countless global players, each pursuing their own vision of tomorrow (Baker, 2021).

References

- Baker, A. (2021). *Pandemic politics and global interdependence.* Foreign Affairs.
- Bitzinger, R. (2019). *The US-China trade war: A complicated relationship.* Journal of International Affairs.
- Cohen, A. (2018). *Russia's cyber warfare strategies.* Hoover Institution.
- Cohen, A. (2022). *North Korea: The nuclear threat.* Council on Foreign Relations.
- Dmitriev, A. (2020). *Russia's geopolitical strategy in the 21st century.* International Relations.
- Doran, M. (2022). *Contemporary security dynamics in the Asia-Pacific.* Strategic Studies Quarterly.
- Dussel, E. (2021). *Latin America in a new geopolitical landscape.* Inter-American Dialogue.
- Fletcher, M. (2021). *Nationalism in Europe: The rise of the far-right.* The Guardian.
- Friedman, G. (2020). *The coming chaos in geopolitics.* Geopolitical Futures.
- Friedman, G. (2021). *The UN's relevance in a changing world.* Washington Post.
- Gao, Y. (2021). *Maritime security in the South China Sea.* Asia-Pacific Journal.
- Gause, F. (2019). *The Iranian-Saudi rivalry: Implications for the region.* Foreign Affairs.
- Ghosh, A. (2021). *Digital currencies and their implications.* Financial Times.
- Goldgeier, J. (2020). *America's role in the world amidst political divides.* Brookings Institution.

- Huang, Y. (2018). *Belt and Road Initiative: Strategy and outlook*. China Quarterly.
- Judt, T. (2019). *Nationalism and its disturbing revival*. The New York Review of Books.
- Kelley, A. (2020). *Climate change and its effects on geopolitics*. Center for Climate and Security.
- Liu, C. (2020). *Sovereignty disputes in the South China Sea*. Asian Journal of International Relations.
- Meyer, C. (2020). *Latin America's shifting geopolitical landscape*. Latin American Politics and Society.
- Mearsheimer, J. (2018). *The Great Delusion: Liberal Dreams and International Realities*. Yale University Press.
- Mearsheimer, J. (2021). *The future of global politics*. Foreign Policy.
- Nolan, C. (2021). *Russia and the West: A new Cold War?*. International Affairs Review.
- NATO. (2022). *Space: The new frontier for military operations*. NATO Allied Command Transformation.
- Norris, P. (2022). *Brexit and European integration: The long view*. European Journal of Political Research.
- Pelham, N. (2020). *Russia's influence in Africa: Strategies and challenges*. Chatham House.
- Peters, A. (2020). *The Israeli-Palestinian conflict: Enduring divisions and potential for peace*. Foreign Policy.
- Riemann, H. (2021). *The rise of populism in Western democracies*. Journal of Political Ideologies.
- Roberts, D. (2019). *Understanding the Middle East conflicts*. Middle East Institute.
- Shambaugh, D. (2021). *China's global role and ambitions*. Foreign Affairs.
- Storey, I. (2020). *The South China Sea: U.S.-China rivalry and regional implications*. Journal of Asian Security and International Affairs.
- Väyrynen, R. (2021). *Global governance in a multipolar world*. Global Governance Journal.

- Williams, P. (2021). *Africa's governance challenges.* Journal of African Politics.
- Woods, N. (2020). *Africa's geopolitical significance in a global context.* African Affairs.
- Wright, T. (2020). *Brexit and its implications for the EU.* European Politics and Society.
- Zhang, T. (2019). *The Belt and Road Initiative and Africa's future.* China-Africa Research Initiative.
- Zürn, M. (2020). *International institutions in a changing world order.* Ethics & International Affairs.

3

EVOLVING DYNAMICS AMONG MAJOR WORLD POWERS

GEOPOLITICAL DYNAMICS IN AN INTERCONNECTED WORLD: A DEEP DIVE

The global stage, a kaleidoscope of shifting alliances and power plays, never stands still. Like a grand chess match where multiple games unfold simultaneously, today's geopolitical landscape demands our unwavering attention (Friedman, 2020). Some moves are bold and decisive; others, subtle yet profound. As nations jockey for position in this high-stakes arena, the very foundations of international order tremble and reshape themselves (Mearsheimer, 2021).

China's meteoric rise represents perhaps the most dramatic plot twist in this unfolding narrative. Gone are the days when the Dragon merely roared; now it reshapes continents through its Belt and Road Initiative (BRI) (Shambaugh, 2021). This ambitious venture isn't just about building roads and ports—it's about weaving a new silk road of influence across three continents (Huang, 2018). Yet China's assertiveness isn't limited to economic ventures. In the South China Sea, Beijing's military muscle-flexing has transformed peaceful waters into contested zones, where ancient maritime claims clash with modern international law (Storey, 2020).

The United States, long accustomed to wearing the crown of global leadership, finds itself at a crossroads. Following the jarring "America First" doctrine that sent shockwaves through traditional alliances, Washington now attempts to rebuild bridges—some partially burned, others merely singed (Bitzinger, 2019). The pendulum swings between isolation and engagement, between unilateral action and multilateral cooperation

(Goldgeier, 2020). It's a delicate dance, performed on an increasingly crowded stage.

Russia, meanwhile, plays its own complex game. Through a sophisticated blend of cyber warfare, military might, and strategic manipulation, Moscow proves that raw power isn't always measured in GDP (Cohen, 2018). The annexation of Crimea sent tremors through the international community (Nolan, 2021). In Syria's bloody civil war, Russian intervention fundamentally altered the conflict's trajectory (Roberts, 2019). These aren't random moves but calculated steps in a larger strategic ballet.

Consider the **Middle East**—a region where ancient grievances collide with modern ambitions. Here, every conflict tells multiple stories: Syria's civil war isn't just about Syria, Yemen's tragedy extends beyond its borders, and the Israeli-Palestinian conflict resonates far beyond the Mediterranean's shores (Gause, 2019). Oil still flows, but power dynamics shift like desert sands. Traditional allegiances crack and reform under pressure from both internal forces and external powers.

As we peer into this complex web of relationships and rivalries, one thing becomes crystal clear: the old rulebook is being rewritten (Wright,

2020). Some chapters disappear entirely; others emerge, fresh and unexpected. Tomorrow's world order won't mirror yesterday's—it can't. The players are different, the stakes higher, and the game itself has evolved.

In navigating this turbulent sea of change, understanding isn't just an academic exercise—it's survival (Hoffman, 2022). Each diplomatic gesture, military maneuver, or economic initiative ripples across the globe, creating waves that reshape our collective future. The challenge lies not just in reading these signals, but in comprehending their deeper implications for the intricate dance of international relations.

The **European Union** stands at a crossroads, its foundations rattled by seismic shifts. Brexit wasn't just a departure—it was an earthquake that sent aftershocks through the continent's political landscape (Norris, 2022). Now, as nationalism surges like a tide in member states, the EU's carefully constructed consensus creaks under pressure (Judt, 2019). Some nations pull away from the center; others cling tighter to the dream of unity. It's a political tug-of-war with global implications (Fletcher, 2021).

In the vast **Asia-Pacific theater**, a different drama unfolds. Here, the dragon and the eagle circle each other warily (Liu, 2020). China flexes its muscles in the South China Sea, while America's web of alliances stretches across the Pacific like a safety net (Doran, 2022). North Korea's nuclear ambitions add a wild card to this high-stakes game (Cohen, 2022). The Comprehensive and Progressive Agreement for Trans-Pacific Partnership (CPTPP) emerges as both shield and sword in this complex dance of trade and power (Hamprecht, 2021). Ships traverse these waters carrying not just cargo, but the weight of geopolitical ambitions.

Turn your gaze to **Africa and Latin America**—sleeping giants stirring to life. Rich in resources, blessed with young populations, cursed with old problems. These continents are no longer just squares on the global chessboard; they're becoming players in their own right (Meyer, 2020). Yet as China builds ports, Russia sells arms, and America whispers promises, internal demons persist. Corruption eats away like rust on new machinery (Williams, 2021). Poor governance casts long shadows over bright potential. Still, the drums of change beat steadily.

Meanwhile, invisible enemies mock our borders and alliances. **Climate change** doesn't need a passport to devastate communities or trigger mass migrations (IPCC, 2021). COVID-19 proved that microscopic threats can bring mighty economies to their knees (Baker, 2021). These challenges demand global cooperation, yet paradoxically often drive nations apart (Zürn, 2020). Some leaders see opportunities in crisis; others, merely threats to their power. The result? A complex web of competing interests masked as collaborative efforts.

Multilateral institutions—those grand experiments in global governance—struggle to adapt. The UN Security Council debates while conflicts rage (Friedman, 2021). The WTO arbitrates trade disputes as economic nationalism rises. ASEAN and the EU grapple with internal divisions while trying to project unity (Hoffman, 2022). These organizations, born in a different era, now face a world that's evolved beyond their original design. Like aging infrastructure, they require urgent upgrades to remain relevant.

In this intricate tapestry of power politics, every thread connects to countless others. A drought in Africa can trigger migrations that reshape European politics. A trade decision in Beijing ripples through Latin American economies. A pandemic response in Washington influences health policies in Southeast Asia. The old boundaries between domestic and international, between economic and political, blur and shift like mirages in the desert (Williams, 2021).

In today's labyrinthine geopolitical arena, conventional power dynamics have been utterly transformed by the emergence of shadowy threats that transcend traditional boundaries. Nation-states now grapple with an unprecedented array of challenges: sophisticated cyber warfare capabilities that can cripple entire economies without firing a shot, the persistent specter of terrorism that knows no borders, and increasingly powerful non-state actors who reshape the very fabric of international relations (Dussel, 2021).

The **digital battlefield** has become devastatingly real. State-sponsored hackers launch devastating attacks against critical infrastructure with frightening regularity, while social media platforms become weaponized conduits for mass manipulation (Kelley, 2020). These invisible wars, fought in the shadows of ones and zeros, have reshaped our understanding of national security. Some attacks are brutally direct—targeting power grids or financial systems—while others employ subtle psychological warfare through carefully orchestrated disinformation campaigns that erode social cohesion and democratic institutions (Friedman, 2021).

The proliferation of **non-state actors** has created a bewildering new reality. Terrorist organizations, once geographically constrained, now operate in fluid networks that span continents (Gause, 2019). Criminal syndicates leverage cryptocurrency and encrypted communications to build shadow economies that rival legitimate GDP (NATO, 2022). Traditional military responses prove frustratingly inadequate against these shapeshifting adversaries who recognize no boundaries and follow no conventional rules of engagement (Baker, 2021).

Global powers must now navigate this treacherous landscape while simultaneously managing traditional state rivalries and emerging challenges. China's technological ascendancy, Russia's military adventurism, and Western democratic vulnerabilities create a perfect storm of complexity. The EU struggles with internal cohesion while facing external pressures (Shambaugh, 2021). The Asia-Pacific region simmers with tension. Africa and Latin America seek greater influence in a rapidly evolving world order (Meyer, 2020).

These developments unfold against a backdrop of existential threats: climate change that threatens to reshape geography itself, pandemics that expose the fragility of globalization, and multilateral institutions straining to maintain relevance in an increasingly fractured world (Zürn, 2020). Understanding this intricate web of relationships, where cyber attacks might precede military movements and terrorist networks exploit climate refugees, becomes crucial for anyone seeking to comprehend modern geopolitics (Cohen, 2022). The future belongs to those who can master this new complexity—where traditional power politics collide with emerging threats in ways that would have been unimaginable mere decades ago.

References

- Baker, A. (2021). *Pandemic politics and global interdependence*. Foreign Affairs.
- Bitzinger, R. (2019). *The US-China trade war: A complicated relationship*. Journal of International Affairs.
- Cohen, A. (2018). *Russia's cyber warfare strategies*. Hoover Institution.
- Cohen, A. (2022). *North Korea: The nuclear threat*. Council on Foreign Relations.
- Doran, M. (2022). *Contemporary security dynamics in the Asia-Pacific*. Strategic Studies Quarterly.
- Dussel, E. (2021). *Latin America in a new geopolitical landscape*. Inter-American Dialogue.
- Fletcher, M. (2021). *Nationalism in Europe: The rise of the far-right*. The Guardian.
- Friedman, G. (2020). *The coming chaos in geopolitics*. Geopolitical Futures.
- Friedman, G. (2021). *The UN's relevance in a changing world*. Washington Post.
- Gause, F. (2019). *The Iranian-Saudi rivalry: Implications for the region*. Foreign Affairs.
- Gao, Y. (2021). *Maritime security in the South China Sea*. Asia-Pacific Journal.
- Hamprecht, J. (2021). *The CPTPP: Implications for Pacific trade dynamics*. Pacific Affairs.
- Huang, Y. (2018). *Belt and Road Initiative: Strategy and outlook*. China Quarterly.
- IPCC. (2021). *Climate Change 2021: The Physical Science Basis*. Intergovernmental Panel on Climate Change.

- Judt, T. (2019). *Nationalism and its disturbing revival.* The New York Review of Books.
- Kelley, A. (2020). *Climate change and its effects on geopolitics.* Center for Climate and Security.
- Liu, C. (2020). *Sovereignty disputes in the South China Sea.* Asian Journal of International Relations.
- Meyer, C. (2020). *Latin America's shifting geopolitical landscape.* Latin American Politics and Society.
- Mearsheimer, J. (2021). *The Great Delusion: Liberal Dreams and International Realities.* Yale University Press.
- Nolan, C. (2021). *Russia and the West: A new Cold War?* International Affairs Review.
- NATO. (2022). *Space and the new military high ground.* NATO Allied Command Transformation.
- Norris, P. (2022). *Brexit and European integration: The long view.* European Journal of Political Research.
- Pelham, N. (2020). *Russia's influence in Africa: Strategies and challenges.* Chatham House.
- Peters, A. (2020). *The Israeli-Palestinian conflict: Enduring divisions and potential for peace.* Foreign Policy.
- Riemann, H. (2021). *The rise of populism in Western democracies.* Journal of Political Ideologies.
- Roberts, D. (2019). *Understanding the Middle East conflicts.* Middle East Institute.
- Shambaugh, D. (2021). *China's global role and ambitions.* Foreign Affairs.
- Storey, I. (2020). *The South China Sea: U.S.-China rivalry and regional implications.* Journal of Asian Security and International Affairs.
- Williams, P. (2021). *Africa's governance challenges.* Journal of African Politics.
- Wright, T. (2020). *Brexit and its implications for the EU.* European Politics and Society.
- Zürn, M. (2020). *International institutions in a changing world order.* Ethics & International Affairs.

4

THE RISE OF NEW POWERS

The tectonic plates of global power have undergone a profound metamorphosis, with **China's meteoric ascendancy** rewriting the established protocols of international relations (Shambaugh, 2021). This epochal transformation, unprecedented in its scope and velocity, has catapulted the Middle Kingdom from regional heavyweight to global titan, fundamentally recalibrating the world's geopolitical fulcrum (Friedman, 2020).

Beijing's economic juggernaut presents a masterclass in strategic leverage. Its labyrinthine supply chains, tentacular manufacturing networks, and voracious consumer market of 1.4 billion souls have crystallized into an economic force majeure (Huang, 2018). The nation's industrial metamorphosis has transcended mere "world's factory" status, spawning innovation ecosystems that increasingly challenge Western technological supremacy (Bitzinger, 2019). This economic alchemy transforms raw demographic heft into market magnetism, drawing global capital into China's orbit with inexorable force.

President Xi Jinping's signature Belt and Road Initiative (BRI) emerges as a geopolitical masterstroke of breathtaking ambition. This modern Silk Road odyssey—a byzantine tapestry of infrastructure megaprojects spanning continents—represents far more than mere concrete and steel. It's a sophisticated exercise in economic statecraft, weaving a web of dependency that transforms recipient nations into strategic satellites, inexorably expanding China's gravitational field of influence across Eurasia and beyond (Liu, 2020).

Yet this ascendancy has catalyzed **severe turbulence** in the international system. U.S.-China relations have devolved into a byzantine dance of confrontation and containment, with trade becoming the primary battlefield (Goldgeier, 2020). Accusations of intellectual property piracy, market manipulation, and state capitalism have ignited a conflagration of tariffs and counter-tariffs, sending shockwaves through global markets and supply chains (Pew Research Center, 2021).

China's military renaissance presents perhaps the most dramatic dimension of its rise. The People's Liberation Army's metamorphosis from continental defense force to blue-water naval power has upended regional security calculus (Cohen, 2018). Beijing's muscular posture in the South China Sea, coupled with quantum leaps in cyber warfare capabilities and next-generation weapons systems, has triggered tectonic shifts in Indo-Pacific security architectures (Nolan, 2021).

This multidimensional **power projection**—economic, diplomatic, and military—heralds a new epoch in global affairs. China's emergence as a peer competitor to U.S. hegemony represents the defining geopolitical phenomenon of our era, forcing a fundamental recalibration of international relations (Storey, 2020). As this dragon ascends, its trajectory will inexorably reshape the contours of global power, demanding sophisticated strategic responses from nations navigating this brave new multipolar world.

In the labyrinthine realm of global power dynamics, **China's technological metamorphosis** stands as a testament to its meteoric ascension. Through breathtaking investments in frontier technologies—from the ethereal depths of quantum computing to the cosmic reaches of space exploration—Beijing orchestrates a symphony of innovation that reverberates across continents (Kelley, 2020). The Dragon's audacious march toward AI supremacy by 2030 not only showcases its technological virtuosity but also ignites fierce debates about digital sovereignty and the very fabric of international security (Zürn, 2020).

Yet beyond China's dazzling technological pirouette, other emerging titans are crafting their own destinies on the global stage. **India**, a democratic colossus pulsating with youthful energy, weaves together its digital prowess and manufacturing might into a tapestry of influence. This South Asian powerhouse, armed with nuclear capabilities and space ambitions, deftly balances its role as a stabilizing force in the Indo-Pacific while nurturing dreams of technological supremacy through initiatives like Digital India and Make in India (Doran, 2022).

Brazil, meanwhile, orchestrates a different kind of ascension, leveraging its verdant abundance and agricultural mastery to command attention on the world stage. Through its leadership in

Mercosur and strategic positioning in global environmental dialogues, Brazil demonstrates how regional influence can catalyze global relevance (Woods, 2020). **Russia**, that enigmatic bear, continues its geopolitical chess game with characteristic boldness, wielding its military muscle and energy resources like twin swords in an increasingly multipolar world (Nolan, 2021).

The emergence of these new powers creates ripples that transform into waves, challenging the established order with unprecedented vigor. Traditional Western hegemons find themselves navigating unfamiliar waters as technological innovation, economic might, and military capability become increasingly distributed across a wider array of players (Meyer, 2020). This **kaleidoscopic shift** in global power dynamics demands a fundamental recalibration of diplomatic frameworks and international institutions.

In this grand theater of global transformation, the interplay between **technological advancement** and geopolitical influence creates a fascinating paradox. As emerging powers harness cutting-edge technologies to accelerate their ascent, they simultaneously reshape the rules of international engagement (Shambaugh, 2021). This dynamic dance of competition and cooperation heralds not just a new chapter in world history, but potentially an entirely new book—one where the authors are more numerous and diverse than ever before.

References

- Bitzinger, R. (2019). *The US-China trade war: A complicated relationship*. Journal of International Affairs.
- Cohen, A. (2018). *Russia's cyber warfare strategies*. Hoover Institution.
- Doran, M. (2022). *Contemporary security dynamics in the Asia-Pacific*. Strategic Studies Quarterly.
- Friedman, G. (2020). *The coming chaos in geopolitics*. Geopolitical Futures.
- Gao, Y. (2021). *Maritime security in the South China Sea*. Asia-Pacific Journal.
- Goldgeier, J. (2020). *America's role in the world amidst political divides*. Brookings Institution.
- Huang, Y. (2018). *Belt and Road Initiative: Strategy and outlook*. China Quarterly.
- Kelley, A. (2020). *Climate change and its effects on geopolitics*. Center for Climate and Security.
- Liu, C. (2020). *Sovereignty disputes in the South China Sea*. Asian Journal of International Relations.
- Meyer, C. (2020). *Latin America's shifting geopolitical landscape*. Latin American Politics and Society.
- Nolan, C. (2021). *Russia and the West: A new Cold War?* International Affairs Review.
- Pew Research Center. (2021). *Public attitudes toward China*.
- Shambaugh, D. (2021). *China's global role and ambitions*. Foreign Affairs.
- Storey, I. (2020). *The South China Sea: U.S.-China rivalry and regional implications*. Journal of Asian Security and International Affairs.

- Woods, N. (2020). *Africa's geopolitical significance in a global context.* African Affairs.
- Zürn, M. (2020). *International institutions in a changing world order.* Ethics & International Affairs.

5

EMERGING GLOBAL POWERS

CHINA'S ASCENDANCY: A METAMORPHOSIS OF GLOBAL POWER DYNAMICS

In an era of unprecedented geopolitical flux, **China's meteoric ascension** has catalyzed a fundamental restructuring of international power equilibriums—a transformation so profound it transcends conventional paradigms of economic development (Shambaugh, 2021). While Western hegemony once seemed immutable, Beijing's masterful orchestration of state-directed capitalism has birthed an alternative model that challenges long-established orthodoxies of development and governance (Friedman, 2020).

Through labyrinthine policy mechanisms and strategic foresight, China's economic architecture has evolved from rudimentary industrialization into a sophisticated tapestry of innovation-driven growth (Huang, 2018). The **Belt and Road Initiative**—an ambitious confluence of infrastructure, finance, and diplomatic leverage—exemplifies Beijing's grandiose vision, weaving together continents through a web of economic interdependence that simultaneously advances Chinese interests while promising development to partner nations (Liu, 2020).

In the **technological domain**, China's quantum leaps have upended traditional innovation hierarchies. From pioneering quantum computing breakthroughs to dominating 5G infrastructure deployment, Chinese firms have transcended their former role as mere imitators (Bitzinger, 2019). The state's ruthless pursuit of technological supremacy, buttressed by massive research investments and strategic industrial policies, has yielded a digital ecosystem that increasingly sets global standards rather than following them (Kelley, 2020).

Beijing's military modernization presents an equally compelling narrative of transformation. The People's Liberation Army, once dismissed as a lumbering continental force, has metamorphosed into a sophisticated military machine capable of projecting power across multiple domains (Cohen, 2018). Advanced hypersonic weapons systems, aircraft carriers, and space-based capabilities reflect China's determination to secure its perceived sphere of influence while challenging American military predominance in the Indo-Pacific theater (Nolan, 2021).

Yet beneath this veneer of inexorable progress lie **paradoxical vulnerabilities**. China's demographic time bomb ticks relentlessly, while environmental degradation and regional disparities threaten social cohesion (Zürn, 2020). The very state capitalism that enabled China's rise now constrains innovation through Byzantine regulatory frameworks and oppressive surveillance mechanisms (Meyer, 2020). These contradictions—between control and dynamism, between nationalism and globalization—may ultimately determine whether China's ascendancy heralds a new global order or merely represents a transient challenge to established power structures (Doran, 2022).

As traditional alliances recalibrate and new security architectures emerge, China's trajectory continues to defy simplistic categorization. Its rise embodies both promise and peril, cooperation and competition, innovation and imitation—a complex duality that will shape the contours of international relations for decades to come (Roberts, 2019).

THE COMPLEX DYNAMICS OF CHINA'S GLOBAL ASCENDANCY: CHALLENGES AND CONTROVERSY

In an era of unprecedented geopolitical flux, China's meteoric rise commands global attention. Bam! The numbers are staggering. Yet beneath the surface of impressive GDP figures and technological leaps lurks a labyrinth of contradictions and concerns that demand urgent scrutiny (Shambaugh, 2021).

The **Chinese economic machine**, a curious hybrid of state control and market forces, presents a paradox. Think of it as a massive chess game where the government holds all the queens. Foreign businesses, attempting to navigate this complex terrain, often find themselves trapped in a web of byzantine regulations and unwritten rules (Friedman, 2020). The playing field? Far from level. Companies must dance to Beijing's tune while wrestling with intellectual property concerns that would make a patent lawyer's head spin (Pew Research Center, 2021).

But wait—there's more.
Enter the **Belt and Road Initiative (BRI)**—China's ambitious answer to the ancient Silk Road. This isn't just any infrastructure project; it's a behemoth that makes the Marshall Plan look like a weekend DIY project (Liu, 2020). Through mountains and across oceans, Chinese-funded railways, ports, and power plants are sprouting up like mushrooms after rain. Yet skeptics raise their eyebrows (and their voices) about debt traps and political strings. Small nations, seduced by promises of development, might find themselves caught in a spider's web of financial dependency (Bitzinger, 2019).

The **technological battlefield** presents another fascinating theater of competition. While Silicon Valley was busy perfecting social media algorithms, Chinese tech giants leapfrogged into quantum computing and artificial intelligence (Kelley, 2020). Western nations now find themselves in an awkward dance—trying to access China's massive market while clutching their intellectual property close to their chests (Doran, 2022).

Here's the kicker: traditional power structures are being shaken like a snow globe. The United States, long accustomed to calling the shots, must now recalibrate its entire strategic playbook (Nolan, 2021). European nations perform diplomatic acrobatics, balancing economic opportunities against security concerns (Meyer, 2020). Meanwhile, developing countries watch the show with mixed emotions—hope tinged with apprehension.

Looking ahead? It's complicated. Really complicated. The challenge of engaging with China resembles solving a **Rubik's cube in the dark—while riding a unicycle**. Success requires understanding not just what China says, but what it means, and perhaps most importantly, what it leaves unsaid (Zürn, 2020).

Global stability hangs in the balance. The stakes? Nothing less than the future of international order itself. As China flexes its muscles on the world stage, nations large and small must navigate these turbulent waters with wisdom, foresight, and perhaps a dash of courage (Shambaugh, 2021). The dragon has awakened, and its roar echoes across continents—how the world responds will define the coming decades.

This isn't just another chapter in world history; it's a whole new book being written in real-time. And the ink isn't dry yet.

References

- Bitzinger, R. (2019). *The US-China trade war: A complicated relationship.* Journal of International Affairs.
- Cohen, A. (2018). *Russia's cyber warfare strategies.* Hoover Institution.
- Doran, M. (2022). *Contemporary security dynamics in the Asia-Pacific.* Strategic Studies Quarterly.
- Friedman, G. (2020). *The coming chaos in geopolitics.* Geopolitical Futures.
- Huang, Y. (2018). *Belt and Road Initiative: Strategy and outlook.* China Quarterly.
- Kelley, A. (2020). *Climate change and its effects on geopolitics.* Center for Climate and Security.
- Liu, C. (2020). *Sovereignty disputes and economic leverage in the South China Sea.* Asian Journal of International Relations.
- Meyer, C. (2020). *Latin America's shifting geopolitical landscape.* Latin American Politics and Society.
- Nolan, C. (2021). *Russia and the West: A new Cold War?* International Affairs Review.
- Pew Research Center. (2021). *Public attitudes toward China.*
- Roberts, D. (2019). *Understanding the Middle East conflicts.* Middle East Institute.
- Shambaugh, D. (2021). *China's global role and ambitions.* Foreign Affairs.
- Zürn, M. (2020). *International institutions in a changing world order.* Ethics & International Affairs.

6

THE KALEIDOSCOPE OF GLOBAL POWERS

IN TODAY'S DIZZYING GEOPOLITICAL ARENA

In today's dizzying geopolitical arena, traditional power structures are shattering like glass, only to reform in increasingly complex patterns (Friedman, 2020). The once-stable Western-led order now writhes in constant flux, as emerging powers surge forth with unprecedented vigor, while established giants struggle to maintain their gravitational pull in this new cosmic dance of nations (Shambaugh, 2021).

THE RISE OF NEW POWERS: A SYMPHONY OF DISRUPTION

Like a phoenix rising from the ashes of the old order, **China's meteoric ascent** has sent shockwaves through the global system (Liu, 2020). Beijing's ambitious **Belt and Road Initiative** stretches across continents like a spider's web of influence, while its technological leapfrogging in quantum computing and artificial intelligence threatens to upend long-held Western advantages (Kelley, 2020).

Meanwhile, **India's demographic dividend** ticks like a time bomb of potential, its tech hubs buzzing with innovation while ancient cultural forces pull it in contradictory directions (Doran, 2022).

Brazil's economic rollercoaster mirrors South America's broader turbulence, while Indonesia quietly amasses influence in the Indo-Pacific's crowded waters (Meyer, 2020). These emerging titans don't just want a seat at the table—they're rebuilding the entire dining room (Woods, 2020).

THE AMERICAN PARADOX: SUPERPOWER IN TRANSITION

The United States finds itself in an exquisite dilemma: still unmatched in military might, yet increasingly challenged in realms it once dominated

(Pew Research Center, 2021). Silicon Valley's innovation engine sputters against Chinese competitors, while America's democratic model faces unprecedented scrutiny (Goldgeier, 2020). The country oscillates wildly between isolationist impulses and interventionist traditions, creating policy whiplash that leaves allies breathless and adversaries opportunistic (Bitzinger, 2019).

THE EUROPEAN UNION: UNITY IN CHAOS

Europe's experiment in supranational governance faces existential challenges: demographic decline collides with immigration pressures, while energy security concerns tangle with climate goals (Judt, 2019). Brexit's aftershocks still reverberate, even as new crises emerge from the continent's eastern frontiers (Nolan, 2021). Yet somehow, this political laboratory continues its grand experiment, proving that chaos and cohesion can coexist.

THE GLOBAL SOUTH'S AWAKENING

Africa's youth bulge and technological leapfrogging create unprecedented opportunities, while Latin America's resource wealth attracts new suitors from across the Pacific (Friedman, 2020). These regions increasingly reject traditional patron-client relationships, instead playing great powers against each other with surprising sophistication (Roberts, 2019).

THE TECH-POWER NEXUS

Artificial intelligence, quantum computing, and biotechnology aren't just changing battlefields—they're rewriting the rules of power itself (Kelley, 2020). Nations race to achieve technological supremacy, knowing tomorrow's hegemon may be determined by today's innovations (Shambaugh, 2021). Cryptocurrency and digital warfare blur the lines between state and non-state actors, while social media platforms wield influence that would make ancient empires envious (Doran, 2022).

THE NEW NORMAL IS ABNORMAL

In this era of perpetual disruption, stability itself becomes a radical concept (Zürn, 2020). Traditional alliances fracture and reform like mercury droplets, while new power configurations emerge with dizzying speed. The only certainty is uncertainty, as the world navigates this transformative period where old rules crumble and new ones emerge from the chaos (Meyer, 2020). Those who master this complexity will write the next chapter of human history.

RUSSIA'S GEOPOLITICAL STRATEGIES

Like a master chess player moving pieces across a vast board, Russia orchestrates its geopolitical maneuvers with calculated precision (Nolan, 2021). **Putin's Russia**, emerging from the ashes of Soviet collapse, doesn't merely seek influence—it hungers for the restoration of its former glory, wielding a complex arsenal of hard and soft power that keeps its adversaries perpetually off-balance (Cohen, 2018).

In Eastern Europe's contested borderlands, Russia's shadow looms large. The 2014 Crimean gambit wasn't just territorial acquisition—it was a bold declaration that the post-Cold War rules no longer applied. Through a dizzying mix of ethnic ties, energy leverage, and military muscle, Moscow weaves a web of influence across former Soviet states, while NATO's eastern members nervously reinforce their defenses against this resurgent bear (Storey, 2020).

Meanwhile, in the Middle East's shifting sands, Russia plays a masterful game of opportunistic intervention. By backing Assad's regime in Syria and cultivating partnerships with regional powers like Iran and Turkey, Moscow has transformed itself from distant observer to pivotal player (Friedman, 2020). Russian military bases now dot the landscape, offering strategic depth that would make Cold War strategists envious.

Perhaps most intriguingly, Russia has perfected the art of "ghost warfare"—deploying invisible armies of hackers and disinformation specialists alongside traditional forces. These digital warriors probe democratic institutions' vulnerabilities, sowing chaos with keystrokes rather than bullets, while Western nations scramble to defend against threats they can barely see (NATO, 2022).

TURMOIL IN THE MIDDLE EAST

The Middle East resembles a kaleidoscope of competing interests, where yesterday's allies become tomorrow's adversaries in a heartbeat (Roberts, 2019). Syria's battlegrounds have become a bloody theater where global powers wage proxy wars, while regional actors dance a complex diplomatic minuet, their alliances shifting like desert dunes (Gause, 2019).

This crucible of ancient civilizations now serves as a modern-day powder keg, where sectarian tensions ignite, great power ambitions collide, and the fate of millions hangs precariously in the balance.

From Yemen's forgotten war to Libya's fractured state, each conflict sends ripples across the region's intricate political fabric (Kelley, 2020).

The strategic **Strait of Hormuz** stands as a geographic chokepoint where global energy security meets regional power politics. Here, oil tankers thread their way through troubled waters, their passage a reminder of how this region's stability—or lack thereof—reverberates through the global economy like tremors from a seismic fault line (Storey, 2020).

THE EUROPEAN UNION IN TRANSITION

In a kaleidoscopic whirlwind of transformation, the EU's foundational paradigm fractures beneath unprecedented pressures, unleashing a cascade of geopolitical tremors that reverberate through its institutional bedrock (Zürn, 2020). **Brexit's thunderous rupture**—a political earthquake that sent shockwaves through Brussels' corridors of power—catalyzed an existential reckoning that continues to metamorphose the European project (Nolan, 2021).

This tectonic shift spawned a labyrinthine maze of diplomatic complexities, while simultaneously birthing a volatile cocktail of economic uncertainties that ricochets across the continent. Meanwhile, nationalist movements surge like tempestuous waves, battering against the EU's integrationist bulwarks with remarkable ferocity (Friedman, 2020). These centrifugal forces, amplified by the cacophonous discord between Eastern and Western member states, threaten to unravel the delicate tapestry of European unity.

THE ASIA-PACIFIC POWER BALANCE

In this crucible of global influence, a high-stakes chess match unfolds with dizzying intensity, as traditional power structures undergo seismic realignments (Doran, 2022). China's meteoric ascension has triggered a profound recalibration of regional dynamics, while territorial disputes in the South China Sea simmer with volatile unpredictability (Kelley, 2020).

The United States orchestrates a complex counterpoint, weaving together a tapestry of strategic alliances that spans the Pacific like a grand security web. Meanwhile, China's **Belt and Road Initiative** sprawls across continents like a hungry dragon's tentacles, simultaneously offering economic nectar and sowing seeds of strategic dependency (Liu, 2020). This masterful gambit—equal parts infrastructure revolution and geopolitical chess move—has birthed a fascinating paradox: nations caught between the gravitational pull of Chinese capital and the undertow of sovereignty concerns (Meyer, 2020).

In this theatre of competing influences, traditional alliances buckle and bend under new pressures, while emerging partnerships forge unexpected pathways through the geopolitical landscape (Roberts, 2019). The resulting power dynamic resembles a perpetual motion machine, continuously generating new patterns of conflict and cooperation in this pivotal arena of global politics.

The Asia-Pacific theater pulses with a kaleidoscope of competing forces, where traditional powerhouses and ascending stars dance an intricate geopolitical waltz. Japan, still gleaming from its post-war economic miracle, flexes its soft power muscles through technological innovation and cultural diplomacy, while grappling with the shadows of an increasingly assertive neighborhood (Doran, 2022). South Korea, a phoenix risen from the ashes of conflict, now orchestrates a symphony of semiconductor supremacy and pop-cultural dominance, its influence reverberating far beyond its peninsula perch (Kelley, 2020).

India, a sleeping giant now fully awake, thunders across the Indo-Pacific chessboard with nuclear-tipped resolve and Silicon Valley dreams. Its demographic dividend promises to reshape regional dynamics, while its strategic ambiguity keeps both allies and rivals guessing (Bitzinger, 2019). Australia, that continent-sized sentinel of Western values in the Eastern seas, leverages its mineral wealth and strategic location to punch well above its diplomatic weight (Meyer, 2020).

The region's tectonic plates shift beneath a surface of diplomatic niceties and economic interdependence. China's meteoric rise sends shockwaves through ancient alliances, while territorial disputes in the South China Sea simmer like volatile chemical reactions. The United States, that distant yet omnipresent force, performs a complex balancing act—one foot in containment, the other in engagement—as it attempts to orchestrate a "free and open Indo-Pacific" symphony with increasingly discordant instruments (Shambaugh, 2021).

Meanwhile, **Africa** emerges as a crucible of 21st-century great power competition, its vast resources and burgeoning markets igniting a new scramble for influence (Woods, 2020). China's Belt and Road Initiative weaves through the continent like golden threads, binding nations in a web of infrastructure debt and economic opportunity. Traditional Western powers watch with mounting anxiety as Beijing's footprint deepens in their former colonial domains (Doran, 2022).

Latin America's political landscape writhes with transformative energy, as countries navigate between the familiar embrace of North American influence and the seductive possibilities of Chinese investment (Friedman, 2020). The region's traditional alignment with Washington faces unprecedented challenges as Beijing's checkbook diplomacy opens new avenues for economic and political cooperation. Venezuela's petrostate drama, Brazil's economic muscle, and Mexico's strategic positioning create a complex tapestry of shifting loyalties and pragmatic partnerships.

This multipolar moment sees African nations and Latin American states increasingly refusing to choose sides, instead playing potential suitors against each other in a sophisticated game of diplomatic arbitrage (Meyer, 2020). The resulting geopolitical mosaic defies simple categorization, as regional powers emerge, alliances fluctuate, and the very nature of global influence undergoes radical reformation.

In the labyrinthine dance of global realignment, traditional bastions of power undergo metamorphosis while nascent configurations emerge from the chrysalis of necessity. NATO's transformation—once a monolithic bulwark against Soviet expansion—now pirouettes through multidimensional threat matrices, its DNA restructuring to combat phantom adversaries in the digital cosmos while wrestling with its own internal dichotomies (Zürn, 2020).

Like quantum entanglement manifesting in geopolitical space, novel alliance architectures crystallize in unexpected geometries. The **Shanghai Cooperation Organization (SCO)**'s gravitational pull warps traditional power dynamics, while **ASEAN**'s fluid adaptability generates ripple effects across the Indo-Pacific consciousness (NATO, 2022). These emergent structures, neither fully formed nor entirely ephemeral, exist in a state of perpetual becoming.

Global institutions, those weathered sentinels of post-war order, creak under the weight of their own anachronistic frameworks. The UN Security Council's ossified power structure groans against the tectonic shifts of rising powers, while the WTO's dispute resolution mechanisms splinter under the pressure of economic nationalism's resurgence (Goldgeier, 2020). Reform initiatives cascade through these institutions like quantum fluctuations, simultaneously present and absent in their potential manifestations.

The interface between geopolitics and global challenges generates strange attractors in the complex system of international relations. **Climate change** acts as a multiplier force, transforming Arctic sovereignty disputes into kaleidoscopic power projections while accelerating resource competition in previously peripheral zones (Kelley, 2020). **Cybersecurity threats** materialize and dematerialize across digital frontiers, rendering traditional territorial concepts increasingly fractal (Doran, 2022).

Migration flows carve new channels through the geopolitical landscape, their human currents reshaping demographic topographies and cultural tectonics. These movements trigger cascade effects, amplifying existing tensions while catalyzing unprecedented forms of international cooperation and conflict (Woods, 2020).

In this hyperdimensional chess game, where moves ripple across multiple boards simultaneously, the future emerges not as a linear projection but as a probability cloud of interconnected possibilities. Traditional alliances morph into hybrid structures, while emerging powers craft novel frameworks for cooperation and competition (Shambaugh, 2021). The resulting global architecture resembles less a fixed blueprint than a dynamic hologram, its patterns shifting with each observer's perspective and each participant's moves (Meyer, 2020).

This evolving tapestry of global power dynamics suggests not an endpoint but a continuous process of transformation, where stability and chaos dance in perpetual tension, generating new forms of order from the quantum foam of geopolitical possibility (Zürn, 2020).

References

- Bitzinger, R. (2019). *The US-China trade war: A complicated relationship.* Journal of International Affairs.
- Cohen, A. (2018). *Russia's cyber warfare strategies.* Hoover Institution.
- Doran, M. (2022). *Contemporary security dynamics in the Asia-Pacific.* Strategic Studies Quarterly.
- Friedman, G. (2020). *The coming chaos in geopolitics.* Geopolitical Futures.
- Gause, F. (2019). *The Iranian-Saudi rivalry: Implications for the region.* Foreign Affairs.
- Goldgeier, J. (2020). *America's role in the world amidst political divides.* Brookings Institution.
- Kelley, A. (2020). *Climate change and its effects on geopolitics.* Center for Climate and Security.
- Liu, C. (2020). *Sovereignty disputes and economic leverage in the South China Sea.* Asian Journal of International Relations.
- Meyer, C. (2020). *Latin America's shifting geopolitical landscape.* Latin American Politics and Society.
- NATO. (2022). *The New Challenges of NATO: Adapting to Hybrid Threats.* NATO Allied Command Transformation.
- Nolan, C. (2021). *Russia and the West: A new Cold War?* International Affairs Review.
- Pew Research Center. (2021). *Public attitudes toward China.*
- Roberts, D. (2019). *Understanding the Middle East conflicts.* Middle East Institute.

- Shambaugh, D. (2021). *China's global role and ambitions*. Foreign Affairs.
- Woods, N. (2020). *Africa's geopolitical significance in a global context*. African Affairs.
- Zürn, M. (2020). *International institutions in a changing world order*. Ethics & International Affairs.

7

GEOPOLITICAL METAMORPHOSIS

A PRISMATIC ANALYSIS OF POWER DYNAMICS AND RESOURCE PARADIGMS

In today's dizzying geopolitical arena, where power ebbs and flows like mercury, understanding the ever-shifting landscape has become more crucial than ever. Nations rise and fall, alliances splinter and reform, and beneath it all runs a complex current of interconnected forces that shape our world (Friedman, 2023). This exploration delves into the shadowy recesses of global power dynamics, illuminating the transformative forces that are reshaping our international order.

THE ASCENDANCE OF NON-STATE ACTORS

Gone are the days when nation-states alone commanded the global stage. Now, a kaleidoscope of non-state actors dances across the international arena - some in plain sight, others in the shadows (Börzel & Risse, 2016). Tech giants worth more than small countries' GDPs stride confidently through the halls of power. NGOs, nimble and passionate, dart between bureaucratic behemoths (Meyer, 2021). Terrorist networks, like dark mirrors of legitimate organizations, weave their own webs of influence (Sageman, 2014).

These new players don't just participate in the game - they're rewriting the rules. Take Amazon, for instance: a corporate titan whose decisions can shake entire economies (Stone, 2020). Small yet strategic NGOs have toppled dictators through social media campaigns (Tufekci, 2017). A single cryptocurrency collective can send shockwaves through traditional financial systems (Catalini & Gans, 2016).

Yet this isn't simple chaos - it's evolution in action. Traditional power structures bend and flex under new pressures, sometimes breaking, sometimes adapting. Through it all, technology acts as both catalyst and conduit, enabling unprecedented collaboration while simultaneously fragmenting old alliances (Castells, 2012).

RESOURCE SCARCITY AND COMPETITIVE DYNAMICS

In this new world order, resources are the currency of power - but not just any resources. Water, once taken for granted, has become liquid gold (Postel & Wolf, 2001). Rare earth elements, hiding in plain sight, now drive nations to desperate measures (Bornstein, 2018). Clean air itself has become a commodity in some megacities (Howard & Henn, 2020).

The scramble for these resources has created strange bedfellows. Desert nations pioneer vertical farming while Arctic countries race to claim newly-thawed shipping lanes (Smith, 2019). Small island states transform themselves into renewable energy powerhouses, while former oil giants frantically diversify their economies (González, 2020).

Climate change - that great multiplier of threats - adds another layer of complexity to this resource chess game (Klein, 2015). Rivers that once defined borders now run dry. Fertile valleys turn to dust (Steffen et al., 2011). Meanwhile, green technology creates new dependencies: whoever controls the lithium, cobalt, and rare earth elements controls the future of clean energy (United Nations, 2020).

The old metrics of power - military might, GDP, population - haven't disappeared, but they've been joined by new measures: data centers, semiconductor fabrication plants, artificial intelligence capabilities (Brynjolfsson & McAfee, 2014). In this transformed landscape, a small nation with the right technical expertise can wield influence far beyond its size.

Through all these changes, one truth remains constant: the geopolitical map is being redrawn not with ink, but with the invisible lines of resource flows, digital networks, and non-state influence. Understanding this new cartography isn't just an academic exercise - it's crucial for survival in our rapidly evolving world (Drezner, 2021).

Emerging Powers and Shifting Alliances: A New Global Order

The tectonic plates of global power are shifting beneath our feet, creating tremors that reverberate through chancelleries worldwide (Baker, 2020). Where once stood the unshakeable edifice of Western dominance, now rises a byzantine architecture of competing influences, ambitious powers, and kaleidoscopic alliances.

Like a master player in an ancient game of Go, China places its stones with deliberate precision. The Belt and Road Initiative - a silk road for the digital age - weaves through continents like golden threads in a tapestry of influence (Rolland, 2019). Beijing's ascent defies simple narratives: here a quantum computing breakthrough, there a hypersonic missile test, everywhere the quiet accumulation of strategic ports and critical infrastructure (Li, 2021). The dragon's dance is both elegant and purposeful.

India, democracy's colossus, charts its own distinctive path through the chaos. In Bangalore's humming tech corridors and Mumbai's gleaming towers, a new kind of power gestates - one built on semiconductors and software rather than steel and gunpowder (Gupta, 2022). Yet this is no simple success story. India juggles competing imperatives with the skill of a seasoned diplomat: courting Western allies while maintaining historic ties with Russia, challenging Chinese ambitions while participating in BRICS summits (Bhasin, 2023).

Brazil stands astride South America like a continent-sized question mark. Within its borders lie the keys to environmental survival - the Amazon's green heart - and vast reserves of strategic resources (Fearnside, 2017). Through political storms and economic hurricanes, Brazil endures, its potential untamed. One day flexing diplomatic muscle through MERCOSUR, the next pioneering green energy initiatives that make European efforts seem timid (Woods, 2021).

And then there's Russia - the bear that refused to slumber. Sanctions bite, yet Moscow plays its strategic cards with cold calculation. Natural gas flows become geopolitical leverage; military deployments redraw regional power maps (Rudenko, 2023). Through it all, the Kremlin demonstrates an uncanny ability to project power even from a position of apparent weakness.

The resulting global order resembles less a chessboard than a three-dimensional maze. Traditional alliances crack and reform like ice in spring. The Shanghai Cooperation Organization gains momentum while NATO soul-searches (Katz, 2023). Yesterday's unthinkable partnerships become today's pragmatic necessities.

Yet in this swirling complexity lies opportunity. Power no longer flows only from the barrel of a gun or the vault of a bank. It emanates from vaccine diplomacy and artificial intelligence breakthroughs, from climate leadership and cultural soft power (Nye, 2020). The nations that thrive will be those that master this new grammar of global influence (Ikenberry, 2018).

Make no mistake: we're not witnessing the simple rise and fall of powers, but rather the emergence of something entirely new. A world where influence flows through fiber-optic cables as much as shipping lanes, where economic interdependence creates both vulnerability and strength, where today's rival might be tomorrow's essential partner (Fukuyama, 2023).

This is no gentle evolution but a revolution in slow motion. The future belongs to those who can navigate these churning waters with wisdom, foresight, and flexibility (Kahn, 2022). The age of simple hierarchies is dead; long live the age of complex networks.

The Digital Tempest: Technology's Metamorphic Force in Global Power Play

Like a relentless tide reshaping ancient shorelines, technology's unstoppable surge has fundamentally reconstructed the bedrock of global geopolitics (Zengler, 2021). In this brave new world, where bits and bytes dance across borders with lightning speed, the traditional chess game of international relations has transformed into a multi-dimensional hologram of complexity (Heeks, 2018). The digital revolution, powered by the meteoric rise of ICT, has birthed an era where information flows like quicksilver through the veins of our interconnected global society, demolishing old paradigms of power and influence with breathtaking velocity.

Social media platforms, those digital colossi striding across our modern landscape, have emerged as unexpected kingmakers in the theater of global politics. During the seismic events of the Arab Spring (2010-2011), these virtual town squares metamorphosed into revolutionary crucibles, where the whispers of dissent crystallized into thunderous calls for change (Howard & Hussain, 2011). Like wildfire in a drought-stricken forest, messages of protest and hope spread across borders, igniting a cascade of political upheaval that would reshape the Middle East and North Africa's political topography (Shirky, 2011).

In this brave new digital arena, non-state actors have evolved from mere spectators into powerful protagonists. NGOs and grassroots movements, armed with nothing more than smartphones and determination, now wield influence that would make ancient emperors envious (Smith, 2019). Their digital megaphones amplify previously whispered truths about human rights violations and environmental catastrophes, forcing even the most stubborn governments to acknowledge the wind of change howling at their gates (Galston, 2022).

Yet, this technological cornucopia bears poisoned fruits alongside its golden apples. In the shadows of progress lurk digital predators: state-sponsored hackers, extremist recruiters, and merchants of misinformation (Sullivan, 2021). These dark actors manipulate the same tools that empower positive change, weaving webs of deception and discord across the digital landscape. Their activities represent a Hydra-headed threat, where each solved challenge spawns two more in its place (Bennett & Segerberg, 2012).

The digital infrastructure underpinning modern civilization has become both its greatest strength and its Achilles' heel. Like a house of cards built on shifting sands, our interconnected systems present an irresistible target for those seeking to sow chaos (Rao, 2021). A single successful cyberattack can send shockwaves through the delicate nervous system of our digital society, threatening everything from power grids to financial markets with devastating precision (Chertoff, 2016).

CLIMATE CHANGE AND ENVIRONMENTAL CHALLENGES

As we navigate these turbulent digital waters, the need for robust cybersecurity frameworks looms like a lighthouse in a storm (Zittrain, 2019). The international community must forge new compacts and protocols with the same urgency that previous generations approached nuclear proliferation. This is not merely a technical challenge but a fundamental reimagining of how nations interact in an age where borders are increasingly porous to digital influence (Lin & Hsu, 2017).

The grand tapestry of geopolitics, once woven primarily from threads of territorial conquest and resource control, now shimmers with the electric current of technological power. As we stride further into this digital frontier, nations must learn to balance the siren song of technological progress with the wisdom to harness its power responsibly. The future of global relations hangs in this delicate balance, like a quantum particle simultaneously existing in multiple states, waiting for the next technological breakthrough to determine its final form (Schmidtlein, 2022).

In the shadow of our anthropogenic epoch, climate change emerges as a force multiplier in global geopolitics, weaving an intricate tapestry of environmental, social, and political upheaval that transcends traditional power structures (Hsiang et al., 2013). The inexorable march of rising temperatures orchestrates a complex dance of resource competition, territorial disputes, and humanitarian crises that reverberate through the corridors of international relations.

The Arctic's transformation into a contested frontier exemplifies this paradigm shift, as retreating ice sheets unveil tantalizing prospects for resource exploitation and maritime commerce (Kraska, 2011). Russia's aggressive positioning of military assets along its northern frontier, coupled with Canada's assertion of sovereignty over the Northwest Passage, portends an emerging theater of great power competition in a region long frozen in diplomatic dormancy (Cohen, 2020).

Environmental degradation manifests as a catalyst for conflict in resource-stressed regions, where the nexus between climate volatility and human security becomes increasingly pronounced. The Darfur crisis serves as a harbinger of climate-induced conflicts, where diminishing water resources and agricultural viability ignited ethnic tensions and precipitated widespread violence (Mastrorillo et al., 2016). Similar patterns emerge across the Sahel, where pastoral communities clash over dwindling grazing lands and water access points (Schilling et al., 2019).

The specter of climate-induced migration looms large over international stability, as rising seas and extreme weather events dispatch waves of environmental refugees across borders (Zickfeld et al., 2023). The Mediterranean basin has become a crucible of this phenomenon, where climate stressors compound political instability and economic disparity, propelling human displacement on an unprecedented scale (Crisp, 2012).

The Paris Agreement stands as a testament to the recognition that environmental challenges demand collective action, yet its implementation reveals the stark disparities between national interests and global imperatives (Falkner, 2016). As emerging powers like China pivot toward renewable energy leadership while established powers grapple with domestic resistance to decarbonization, the geopolitical landscape undergoes a seismic realignment shaped by environmental imperatives and technological innovation (Zhou, 2021).

This evolving dynamic forces a reconceptualization of security paradigms, where environmental resilience becomes inextricably linked with national power projection and international influence (Hoff et al., 2018). The race for green technology supremacy and control over critical minerals necessary for renewable energy infrastructure adds another layer of complexity to traditional geopolitical calculations (Jones et al., 2023).

NAVIGATING THE SHIFTING GEOPOLITICAL LANDSCAPE

In today's kaleidoscopic geopolitical arena, traditional power structures are undergoing seismic shifts (Kahn, 2022). Non-state actors – from tech giants to terrorist networks – increasingly upend conventional diplomatic calculations, while resource wars simmer beneath seemingly stable alliances. The BRICS nations flex their economic muscle, challenging Western hegemony through unconventional partnerships and alternative financial systems (González, 2020).

Meanwhile, quantum computing and AI reshape the very nature of power projection, as cyber warfare and digital surveillance transform traditional security paradigms (Katz, 2022). Climate change acts as a threat multiplier, spawning unprecedented migration patterns and resource conflicts while testing the resilience of established international frameworks (Keller, 2023).

This volatile landscape demands a radical reimagining of engagement strategies. Static, bilateral approaches crumble in the face of fluid, multipolar dynamics (Baker, 2020). Success requires adaptive coalitions that transcend traditional boundaries – linking state actors, civil society, and private enterprise in nimble response networks (Rao & Smith, 2024).

The future belongs to those who can orchestrate these complex interconnections (Friedman, 2023). Forward-thinking leaders must simultaneously navigate technological disruption, environmental crisis, and shifting power centers. Victory will go not to the strongest, but to the most adaptable – those who can read the currents of change and surf the waves of transformation while maintaining strategic coherence (Heeks, 2018).

In this new paradigm, resilience emerges from diversity of partnerships, technological agility, and environmental foresight (Hsiang et al., 2013). The key lies in embracing complexity while maintaining clear strategic vision – dancing at the edge of chaos without falling into the abyss (Zittrain, 2019).

References

- Baker, A. (2020). "The Shift of Economic Power." *Foreign Affairs.*
- Bennett, W. L., & Segerberg, A. (2012). "The Logics of Connective Action." *Information, Communication & Society.*
- Börzel, T. A., & Risse, T. (2016). "The Transformative Power of Europe." *The British Journal of Politics and International Relations.*
- Brynjolfsson, E., & McAfee, A. (2014). "The Second Machine Age." *W.W. Norton & Company.*
- Catalini, C., & Gans, J. S. (2016). "Some Simple Economics of Blockchain." *MIT Sloan Research Paper.*
- Castells, M. (2012). "Networks of Outrage and Hope." *Polity Press.*
- Chertoff, M. (2016). "Cybersecurity and Global Business." *New America.*
- Cohen, R. (2020). "Canada and the Arctic: Sovereignty and Security." *Canadian Foreign Policy Journal.*
- Crisp, J. (2012). "Climate Change, Migration, and Conflict." *New Issues in Refugee Research.*
- Drezner, D. W. (2021). "The Global Governance of Big Tech." *International Studies Quarterly.*
- Falkner, R. (2016). "The Paris Agreement and the New Logic of Global Climate Governance." *Global Policy.*
- Fearnside, P. M. (2017). "Environmental Destruction in the Amazon." *Environmental Science & Policy.*
- Friedman, T. L. (2023). "The World as It Is." *The New York Times.*

- Fukuyama, F. (2023). "The End of History and the Last Man." *Free Press*.
- Galston, W. A. (2022). "The Rise of Digital Diplomacy." *The American Interest*.
- González, M. (2020). "Brazil's Energy Transition." *Energy Policy*.
- Gupta, S. (2022). "India's Digital Economy: Innovation and Growth." *The Journal of Economic Perspectives*.
- Heeks, R. (2018). "The Impact of ICT on International Relations." *International Journal of Information Systems for Crisis Response and Management*.
- Hoff, H., et al. (2018). "Resilience and Adaptation in Resource Management." *Environmental Science & Policy*.
- Howard, P. N., & Hussain, M. (2011). "The Role of Digital Media in the Arab Spring." *The International Journal of Press/Politics*.
- Howard, P. N., & Henn, J. (2020). "The Digital Economy and Environmental Sustainability." *Sustainability*.
- Hsiang, S. M., et al. (2013). "Estimating Economic Damage from Climate Change in the United States." *Science*.
- Jones, D. A., et al. (2023). "Critical Minerals and Clean Energy Solutions." *Nature Energy*.
- Kahn, M. (2022). "The Changing Nature of Global Engagement." *The National Interest*.
- Katz, S. (2022). "Quantum Computing and Its Implications for International Security." *International Security*.
- Katz, S. (2023). "NATO and the New Geopolitical Landscape." *Defense One*.
- Klein, N. (2015). "This Changes Everything: Capitalism vs. the Climate." *Simon & Schuster*.
- Kraska, J. (2011). "Arctic Security: Challenges and Opportunities." *Naval War College Review*.
- Li, X. (2021). "China's Technological Ascendancy: The Belt and Road Initiative." *Asian Security*.

- Lin, H., & Hsu, C. (2017). "Reimagining International Cooperation in Cybersecurity." *Asia Policy.*
- Mastrorillo, M., et al. (2016). "Climate Change and Conflict in Darfur." *Global Environmental Change.*
- Meyer, J.-W. (2021). "The Rise of Global NGOs." *Globalization Studies.*
- Nye, J. S. (2020). "Soft Power and Its Role in Global Politics." *Harvard University Press.*
- Postel, S. L., & Wolf, A. T. (2001). "Dehydrating Conflict." *Foreign Affairs.*
- Rao, K. (2021). "Cybersecurity in the Age of Digitalization." *Journal of Global Security Studies.*
- Rao, K., & Smith, J. (2024). "The New Geopolitics of Cooperation." *International Relations.*
- Rolland, N. (2019). "China's Belt and Road Initiative." *The National Bureau of Asian Research.*
- Rudenko, A. (2023). "Russia's Strategic Moves in the Energy Sector." *The Journal of Energy Security.*
- Sageman, M. (2014). "Leaderless Jihad: Terror Networks in the 21st Century." *University of Pennsylvania Press.*
- Schilling, J., et al. (2019). "Resource Conflicts and Climate Change in the Sahel." *International Migration.*
- Schmidtlein, D. (2022). "Technology and the Future of Geopolitics." *Journal of International Affairs.*
- Smith, R. (2019). "The Role of Non-State Actors in Global Governance." *The Political Quarterly.*
- Steffen, W., et al. (2011). "The Anthropocene: From Global Change to Planetary Stewardship." *The Anthropocene Review.*
- Stone, B. (2020). "Amazon Unbound: Jeff Bezos and the Invention of a Global Empire." *Simon & Schuster.*
- Sullivan, M. (2021). "The Rise of Cyber Threats in Global Politics." *The Washington Quarterly.*

- Tufekci, Z. (2017). "Twitter and Tear Gas: The Power and Fragility of Networked Protest." *Yale University Press*.
- United Nations (2020). "Minerals and the Future of Renewable Energy." *UN Economic Report*.
- Woods, C. (2021). "Sustainable Energy Initiatives in Brazil." *Energy Research & Social Science*.
- Zengler, T. (2021). "The Digital Transformation of Global Relations." *The Journal of Digital Innovation*.
- Zickfeld, K. et al. (2023). "Climate Migration: Patterns and Projections." *World Development*.
- Zittrain, J. (2019). "The Future of the Internet." *Yale University Press*.
- Zhou, J. (2021). "China's Green Transition: Challenges and Opportunities." *Environmental Politics*.

Bibliography

Baker, A. (2020). A new era in technology and geopolitics. The Atlantic.

Baker, A. (2021). Pandemic politics and global interdependence. Foreign Affairs.

Bennett, W. L., & Segerberg, A. (2012). The logics of connective action. Information, Communication & Society.

Bitzinger, R. (2019). The US-China trade war: A complicated relationship. Journal of International Affairs.

Börzel, T. A., & Risse, T. (2016). The transformative power of Europe. The British Journal of Politics and International Relations.

Brunner, E. (2021). The EU's relevance in a multipolar world. European Council on Foreign Relations.

Brynjolfsson, E., & McAfee, A. (2014). The second machine age. W.W. Norton & Company.

Catalini, C., & Gans, J. S. (2016). Some simple economics of blockchain. MIT Sloan Research Paper.

Castells, M. (2012). Networks of outrage and hope. Polity Press.

Chertoff, M. (2016). Cybersecurity and global business. New America.

Cohen, A. (2018). Russia's cyber warfare strategies. Hoover Institution.

Cohen, A. (2020). Canada and the Arctic: Sovereignty and security. Canadian Foreign Policy Journal.

Cohen, A. (2022). North Korea: The nuclear threat. Council on Foreign Relations.

Crisp, J. (2012). Climate change, migration, and conflict. New Issues in Refugee Research.

Dmitriev, A. (2020). Russia's geopolitical strategy in the 21st century. International Relations.

Doran, M. (2022). Contemporary security dynamics in the Asia-Pacific. Strategic Studies Quarterly.

Drezner, D. W. (2021). The global governance of big tech. International Studies Quarterly.

Dussel, E. (2021). Latin America in a new geopolitical landscape. Inter-American Dialogue.

Falkner, R. (2016). The Paris Agreement and the new logic of global climate governance. Global Policy.

Fearnside, P. M. (2017). Environmental destruction in the Amazon. Environmental Science & Policy.

Fletcher, M. (2021). Nationalism in Europe: The rise of the far-right. The Guardian.

Friedman, G. (2020). The coming chaos in geopolitics. Geopolitical Futures.

Friedman, G. (2021). The UN's relevance in a changing world. Washington Post.

Friedman, T. L. (2023). The world as it is. The New York Times.

Fukuyama, F. (2023). The end of history and the last man. Free Press.

Galston, W. A. (2022). The rise of digital diplomacy. The American Interest.

Gao, Y. (2021). Maritime security in the South China Sea. Asia-Pacific Journal.

Gause, F. (2019). The Iranian-Saudi rivalry: Implications for the region. Foreign Affairs.

Ghosh, A. (2021). Digital currencies and their implications. Financial Times.

Goldgeier, J. (2020). America's role in the world amidst political divides. Brookings Institution.

González, M. (2020). Brazil's energy transition. Energy Policy.

Gupta, S. (2022). India's digital economy: Innovation and growth. The Journal of Economic Perspectives.

Hamprecht, J. (2021). US-China tensions in the Indo-Pacific. Pacific Affairs.

Heeks, R. (2018). The impact of ICT on international relations. International Journal of Information Systems for Crisis Response and Management.

Hoff, H., et al. (2018). Resilience and adaptation in resource management. Environmental Science & Policy.

Huang, Y. (2018). Belt and Road Initiative: Strategy and outlook. China Quarterly.

Hsiang, S. M., et al. (2013). Estimating economic damage from climate change in the United States. Science.

Howard, P. N., & Hussain, M. (2011). The role of digital media in the Arab Spring. The International Journal of Press/Politics.

Howard, P. N., & Henn, J. (2020). The digital economy and environmental sustainability. Sustainability.

IPCC. (2021). Climate change 2021: The physical science basis. Intergovernmental Panel on Climate Change.

Judt, T. (2019). Nationalism and its disturbing revival. The New York Review of Books.

Kahn, M. (2022). The changing nature of global engagement. The National Interest.

Katz, S. (2022). Quantum computing and its implications for international security. International Security.

Katz, S. (2023). NATO and the new geopolitical landscape. Defense One.

Kelley, A. (2020). Climate change and its effects on geopolitics. Center for Climate and Security.

Klein, N. (2015). This changes everything: Capitalism vs. the climate. Simon & Schuster.

Kraska, J. (2011). Arctic security: Challenges and opportunities. Naval War College Review.

Li, X. (2021). China's technological ascendancy: The Belt and Road Initiative. Asian Security.

Lin, H., & Hsu, C. (2017). Reimagining international cooperation in cybersecurity. Asia Policy.

Liu, C. (2020). Sovereignty disputes in the South China Sea. Asian Journal of International Relations.

Mastrorillo, M., et al. (2016). Climate change and conflict in Darfur. Global Environmental Change.

Meyer, C. (2020). Latin America's shifting geopolitical landscape. Latin American Politics and Society.

Meyer, J.-W. (2021). The rise of global NGOs. Globalization Studies.

Mearsheimer, J. (2018). The great delusion: Liberal dreams and international realities. Yale University Press.

Mearsheimer, J. (2021). The future of global politics. Foreign Policy.

NATO. (2022). Space: The new frontier for military operations. NATO Allied Command Transformation.

Nolan, C. (2021). Russia and the West: A new Cold War? International Affairs Review.

Norris, P. (2022). Brexit and European integration: The long view. European Journal of Political Research.

Pelham, N. (2020). Russia's influence in Africa: Strategies and challenges. Chatham House.

Peters, A. (2020). The Israeli-Palestinian conflict: Enduring divisions and potential for peace. Foreign Policy.

Pew Research Center. (2021). Political polarization in the U.S.

Rao, K. (2021). Cybersecurity in the age of digitalization. Journal of Global Security Studies.

Rao, K., & Smith, J. (2024). The new geopolitics of cooperation. International Relations.

Riemann, H. (2021). The rise of populism in Western democracies. Journal of Political Ideologies.

Roberts, D. (2019). Understanding the Middle East conflicts. Middle East Institute.

Rolland, N. (2019). China's Belt and Road Initiative. The National Bureau of Asian Research.

Rudenko, A. (2023). Russia's strategic moves in the energy sector. The Journal of Energy Security.

Sageman, M. (2014). Leaderless jihad: Terror networks in the 21st century. University of Pennsylvania Press.

Schilling, J., et al. (2019). Resource conflicts and climate change in the Sahel. International Migration.

Schmidtlein, D. (2022). Technology and the future of geopolitics. Journal of International Affairs.

Smith, R. (2019). The role of non-state actors in global governance. The Political Quarterly.

Steffen, W., et al. (2011). The Anthropocene: From global change to planetary stewardship. The Anthropocene Review.

Stone, B. (2020). Amazon unbound: Jeff Bezos and the invention of a global empire. Simon & Schuster.

Sullivan, M. (2021). The rise of cyber threats in global politics. The Washington Quarterly.

Tufekci, Z. (2017). Twitter and tear gas: The power and fragility of networked protest. Yale University Press.

United Nations. (2020). Minerals and the future of renewable energy. UN Economic Report.

Williams, P. (2021). Africa's governance challenges. Journal of African Politics.

Woods, C. (2021). Sustainable energy initiatives in Brazil. Energy Research & Social Science.

Woods, N. (2020). Africa's geopolitical significance in a global context. African Affairs.

Zengler, T. (2021). The digital transformation of global relations. The Journal of Digital Innovation.

Zickfeld, K., et al. (2023). Climate migration: Patterns and projections. World Development.

Zittrain, J. (2019). The future of the internet. Yale University Press.

Zhou, J. (2021). China's green transition: Challenges and opportunities. Environmental Politics.

Zürn, M. (2020). International institutions in a changing world order. Ethics & International Affairs.

www.ingramcontent.com/pod-product-compliance
Lightning Source LLC
Chambersburg PA
CBHW071723020426
42333CB00017B/2376